Pro GOD'S way

Don't bury it in the ground

III John 2
...I wish above all things
that you may prosper...

James R. Whitmer

Prosperity God's Way

First printing July 2023

Another amateur produced spare bedroom publication of:
James R Whitmer
2521 NW 1124 Terrace
Oklahoma City, OK 73120
j.whitmer@cox.net   Land line, 405-751-4521

Also available online through Amazon/Kindle download.

Library of Congress Control Number: 2023913387
International Standard Book Number: 979-8-218-95889-3

The King James Translation of the Bible is used so I don't have to pay royalties to today's Scribes who produce current translations. Some scriptures are composed by the author's personal paraphrase.

Produced in The U S A by American workers.
Publishing rights: FOR SALE !

CONTENTS

INTRODUCTION

It is the belief of this writer that our God Of The Holy Trinity wants us to prosper so that we can fund the ministries involved in His current end time harvest of souls. He has appointed as His Ambassadors those who are an attraction to Christianity, not a promotion of it. Well dressed, well mannered, neat, clean, upscale and attractive, representing The Lord Jesus in a first-class way, the way all Ambassadors should appear as they give credit and praise to one who appointed them to such a prestigious position. Who would want an Ambassador dressed in cheap, unattractive clothes, driving a near junk or dirty vehicle, living on middle to low income? Satan himself, that's who.

Having received a profound conversion to the Christian faith in 1976, I discovered the Bible prosperity message. It sprung up as a somewhat new doctrine at that time. I listened closely to the TV and Radio Preachers. I knew some of what I heard was valid, but I also knew some of the preachers butchered Malachi 3: 8-10. They turned hundreds of thousands of people away from God's desire that **above all things** He wants His children to prosper, to be in good health even as their souls prosper (III John 2). I decided **the prosperity message applies to us today** if we can properly unravel and implement it. That's exactly what this book is about. Its main purpose is to help others prosper financially and carry forward the causes of our Lovely Lord Jesus. It has been my banking experience that if done properly, you will prosper, just like many of us. Those who criticize the doctrine are just not doing it right. Today I enjoy an abundant life of success of which I had only dreamed. God gets the credit. All I did was **what He tells us to do**. It took study and trust. I hope this writing will increase your trust, shorten your study, and **fatten up your soon to come tithe, offering and gift account ! !**

FOR I KNOW THE PLANS I HAVE FOR
YOU, SAYS THE LORD, PLANS TO
PROSPER YOU, AND NOT FOR EVIL,
TO GIVE YOU A FUTURE AND A HOPE.
Jeremiah 29:11

HE SHALL BE LIKE A TREE PLANTED
BY THE RIVERS OF WATER, THAT
BRINGS FORTH FRUIT...... AND WHAT
SO EVER HE DOES **SHALL PROSPER**.
Psalms 1;3

.....THE **WEALTH** OF THE NATIONS
SHALL COME TO YOU.
Isaiah 60:5

IF THEY LISTEN AND **SERVE HIM,**
THEY COMPLETE THEIR DAYS IN
PROSPERITY, AND THEIR YEARS IN
PLEASANTNESS.
Job 36:11

THE **WEALTH** OF THE WICKED IS
LAID UP FOR THE JUST.
Proverbs 13:22

HE GIVES POWER TO GET **WEALTH**
Deuteronomy 8:18

CHAPTER 1

CANCEL THE CURSE

The Old Testament manuscripts were originally written in the Hebrew language. Most of the New Testament was originally written in the Greek language. God's translated words can be complicated. It's difficult to absorb in some areas. Such is the case with the basis for this writing. When we pray for guidance and use dictionaries, usually we can come to a comfortable interpretation. It often takes more than a casual effort but in the end, understanding will come. With Malachi 3: 8-10 not only understanding but cold hard cash. Read on please.

MALACHI 3: 8-10

8 Will a man rob God? Yet you have robbed me! But you say, in what way have we robbed You? In tithes and offerings.

9 You *are** **cursed** with a **curse,** for you have robbed Me, *even* this whole nation.

10 Bring all the tithes into the storehouse,** that there may be meat*** in My house, and prove me now in this says the Lord of hosts, if I will not open for you the windows of heaven and pour out for you *such* a blessing, that *there shall* not *be room* enough *to receive it.*

How do we cancel the **curse** in verse 9? The following will not be the most attractive portion of this writing. It will perhaps be the least attractive but in many areas, there is no way out of life's traps other than obedience to God's instructions. No other way! While you may **not** be able to implement the **curse canceling** procedure outlined in the next few paragraphs, we can consider them and have them **put up on the shelf** so to speak, ready to plunge forward with them at a later date and bring about 100% **elimination** of both **curses** described in Malachi 3:9.

Before we go on let's see if we can establish a simple definition of the word **curse.** To me it's like something negative happening regularly and frequently. In the case of Malachi, money is involved with the specific **curse.** So I will assume negative happenings are going to occur financially until the curse is **canceled.** Negative aspects you may ask. What type of negative aspects? Losing money might be exactly what is being described. To eliminate such occurrences, first we have to admit that not **returning the tithe** is a sin. Sin brings sickness disease **poverty** and death. Yuck! The specific sin of not tithing brought the specific curse. Same with not making offerings. It's sin and the specific sin brought that specific curse. To cancel the curse, we confess the sin, and fervently ask for forgiveness and stop the non-tithing and the zero-offering activity. Then make a pledge and keep it. I pledged 12 to 15% years ago and today I'm doing quite well and have for many-many years now as a businessman and later as an employer.

All of the above seems to boil down to this: God will kick our tail or prosper us, one or the other. I unknowingly chose prosperity and wow am I ever glad I did. Do you suspect that God prompted me in that direction years ago? I do! I suspect it. I did not say He did it. I say I suspected it.

See explanations on page 87 concerning italicized words in the King James translation of the Bible.

** *Storehouse: From the Hebrew Bible dictionary; reference #214; "treasury"*

*** *See several dictionary definitions of the word "meat" on page 91.*

He left the 99 to rescue me!

CHAPTER 2

TWO ROBBERIES
TAKE PLACE

Two robberies are taking place. One is the robbing of tithes. The other is the robbing of offerings. When the preachers nag at us to give more money, they usually lump both the robberies into one occurrence. Malachi mentions two different responses coming from God. The first response is "open windows." The second response is the "pouring out of blessings." The preachers usually lump the two robberies together. Then they lump the two responses together. One response concerns the tithe which God says is going to open windows. The next response comes from the offerings which God says is going to prompt the pouring out of blessings. Time after time I would hear the preachers lump the two responses all together, just like they lump the two robberies together. After some study time I think I figured it out. The first robbery is the **non-return of the tithe.** The tithe has always belonged to God. That 10% never has been mine, and He wants me to **return it** to Him. When I started **returning** the full 10% of my income to Him, which belonged to Him all along, that **return** opened the windows of heaven. Elimination of my first robbery, (**returning the 10th**) prompted the first response from God. His first response is to open heaven's windows, nothing more. God is not going to pour out blessings to me if the only thing I do is **return to Him** the tithe that all along has always been **His.** Why should He pour out a blessing to me if the only thing I do is **return** something to Him that has always been His to begin with? I'll share a comparison story on page 40 of this writing, first paragraph, but first let's look at robbery number two, which is the **non-payment** of offerings. Notice that I'm using the word **"payment"** now rather than the word **"return."** The payment of offerings will prompt God to implement response number two, which is abundant blessings being poured out thru those windows that God opened as a result of **returning** the tithe. It's just so simple. **The return of His tithe opens the windows of heaven. The offerings prompt the blessings to flow out thru the previously opened windows.** Offerings and tithes are two different things. Opening windows is one thing. Pouring blessings out is another. One is a result of returning the tithe. The other is a result of making offerings. One is the result of canceling curse number one and the other is a result of canceling curse number two. How about that?

He left the 99 to rescue me !

NOTES

CHAPTER 3

ALL MONEY BELONGS TO GOD.

All the gold and all the silver belongs to God. All the money on earth belongs to God. All the cattle (cattle being a world-wide symbol of wealth) belong to God. Anything that is valuable belongs to God. The whole earth and every star in the sky belongs to God.

Regarding money: God makes it available to all mankind for our usage. He does stipulate that 10% of it should be returned to Him. His preference as to where you place the 10th that has been entrusted to you, is outlined in scripture. The specific placement starts an argument that seems never ending. I'm going to avoid the argument in order to make this writing easy to follow. We must believe that the 10th is to be used for the causes of The God of The Holy Trinity. The

10th is the tithe. That's what the word tithe means. The offering is the amount over the tithe. It's the amount over 10%. The tithe has always belonged to God. The offerings come from my resources. It's like God gives us the opportunity to be in partnership with Him. God has promised that if I return to Him the tithe and make offerings from my resources, that by placing both where God instructs, He will pour out blessings toward us. His Church is one place where he instructs us to place tithes and offerings, widows are another place, the fatherless is another place. (which would include struggling single moms) and sojourners (people moving from one country to another) is another place. He has assigned the financial partnership to believers.

To sum up this chapter; the 10% is to be **returned to Him.** The amount we decide to give as an offering is the amount **over 10%.** No tithe is robbery. No offering is robbery. What if I was to rob a bank once a week. What is the difference in that and robbing God on Sunday? No difference. Perhaps to rob God is worse than doing so to a bank once a week. Things in the Bible can be rather frightening. Most all the **fear goes away with obedience.** Vanishing fear and a window flowing with blessings seems to me like 12% to 15% or maybe even 20% is quite the bargain.

He left the 99 to rescue me!

NOTES

CHAPTER 4

WHAT SIZE OFFERING ?

Let's take a look at part of Matthew 7:2 **the measure with which you use to measure out will be used to measure back to you.** It's a very generous thing to give offerings. When I did, very generous blessings came flowing right out of those open windows of Heaven. I liked the idea of that. I had more money **to do things for our Lovely Lord Jesus** based on my gratitude and growing love toward Him. One thing I could do is **support ministries**, especially those who help the poor and suffering. It turns out to be fun! If I told you of all the ministry activities I have funded these past 40 years, based on my generous placement first, then the generosity being poured out thru those windows, coming from God our Father, The Lord Jesus and the

Comforting Holy Spirit, you probably would not believe me. Consider this please. It seems that one purpose of God's prosperity blessing is to **fund more ministry activities**. He wants us to have nice things for ourselves. Nice clothes, nice home, nice cars. It's a witness of prosperity that is attractive to others. They will want what we have. But we cannot go overboard with the self. The financial blessings are not just so we can buy a new Corvette and a Lear Jet. Balance should be implemented.

So I say the same thing Gods says in Malachi. Try it and see for yourself. Put God to the test and see what happens. First ask for forgiveness for not **returning His tithe** in days past. Next ask for strength to **return His tithe** for the rest of your life. Next, regularly **return His tithe,** then make the offerings. Please remember now, if you use a wee little pitcher to pour out your offerings, even though they are based on generosity, God will use a wee little pitcher to pour out His generous blessings thru those opened windows. Who do you think will be the most generous, you or God? If you use a bucket to pour out your generosity, instead of a wee little pitcher, what size bucket full will God use to pour out His generosity back to you? How about using a barrel full? How about a big tanker truck full? This can turn out to be fun! It has been for me.

He left the 99 to rescue me !

NOTES

CHAPTER 5

THE STRONG'S EXHAUSTIVE CONCORDANCE.

If I reference every bible verse that contains the words PROSPER,-------PROSPERED, PROSPERETH,-------------- PROSPERITY, PROSPEROUS, and PROSPEROUSLY from an exhaustive Bible concordance, then we could go to sleep before we could read it all in one setting. Those words are mentioned in 93 different scriptures in the King James translation of the Bible.

Therefore the short-cut method is going to have to involve some faith and trust. Some scholars say faith and trust are one in the same. My trust in God is automatic these days based on how many hundreds of times the abundant life with prosperity has come my way. My abundant life has included abundant cash. My offering was cash. My abundance came back as cash. Isn't that what Jesus is saying in Matthew 7:2 as he says ---- **the measure you use to measure out will be used to measure back to you?** Seemingly it did not come my way even when I was returning the tithe without offerings. It seemed the abundant flow started when I tithed and made offerings combined with His tithe. Not just the tithe alone but when offerings were included, which is the amount above the tithe. Again, as before in this writing: Returning His tithe opens the windows. Seemingly that's all it does. Providing an offering starts the flow of the blessings of abundant life that come through the windows of which the tithe opened. Two entirely different activities. One activity is the opening. The second activity is the flowing of abundance. It has come my way for about 35 years now at a slow but steady flow. Numerous times there has been a whopper positive bump in the flow.

He left the 99 to rescue me !

ADDITIONAL WRITINGS

To fatten up this booklet a little bit, I have included some of my previous writings that relate to this same subject. I hope you enjoy them.

He left the 99 to rescue me !

NOTES

CHAPTER 6

90% BLESSED
OR
100% CURSED ?

Long ago I became interested in the teachings of First Fruits." An Old Testament Covenant establishes the instructions for the first 10% of a harvest to be given to God. When the first 10% is returned, God promised to bless the remaining 90%. There is however a downside to this covenant. A negative will occur if one does not return the first 10%. God will curse the entire 100% if the first 10% is not returned to Him. Many scholars say this covenant remains in place today, which raises the question: Would I rather have 90% of my funds blessed or 100% cursed? I found a good definition for the word "covenant" as follows; **"A binding agreement established by one**

party, offered to another party, who can accept or reject but cannot alter." In short, it's a take it or leave it deal! You may ask, where in the Bible is an example of First Fruits? It is laced into the Book of Joshua. Many have heard the story of Joshua fighting the battle of Jericho. After Moses died, Joshua became the military leader. His objective was the conquest of the land God had promised to Israel. "First fruits" is a big part of this story. God told Joshua that the gold and silver from the plunder of Jericho must go to His Tabernacle Treasury. Joshua was plainly told that the Israelite's were not to take any for themselves just yet. All was to go to the Tabernacle Treasury. Why? Because it was the First Fruits of the first of many plunder yielding battles to come. If Israel violated the covenant of "First Fruits" then God would violate my promise and **not bless** the future military efforts. They could all be killed. Joshua knew this. One soldier named Achen did not obey God's instructions. He took gold, silver and a beautiful garment from the plunder of Jericho. He hid the loot in his tent. Then the Lord was angry with the Israelite's. Achen's sin canceled the previous covenant connection to future combat success. The next battle was Ai (pronounced eye). This was a small Kingdom with not much of a military. Joshua sent about 3000 men to attack the much smaller army of Ai, but the Israelite army did not win the battle because God was no longer on their side. Because of their covenant violation of "First Fruits" God would not bless their efforts. Instead God cursed their efforts! This heavily out-numbered weak Ai military chased Joshua's top-notch soldiers out of the area and killed about 36 Israelite soldiers as they retreated.

The Lord spoke to dejected Joshua. He told him that Israel had violated His covenant of "First Fruits." They had stolen a portion of the gold and silver. They also had lied about it and hid the plunder. This is why the Israelite army was defeated by those of Ai. The Lord told the Israelites He would not be with them any longer unless they destroyed some things among themselves. The Lord further instructed Joshua to do a family-by-family search. When it came to Achen, he confessed. The gold and silver was placed in the Treasury and the covenant was re-established. Next was another battle with Ai. This time the Lord was on their side. This time the Lord told them they could keep all the plunder for themselves. Why? Because they had paid the "First Fruits" that came from the battle of Jericho. The Ai plunder was to be kept by the Israelites for themselves. There was a total of 29 more battles to purge Israel of the various Kingdoms which had taken land from Israel. The Israelites did not lose one of the numerous battles and all the plunder of all the battles belonged to them. This completed God's covenant of "First Fruits." What happened to Achen the thief? Based on God's instructions the Isrselites stoned him and all his family to death and burned their bodies prior to the second battle with Ai.

I'm rather comfortable with this story as harsh as it is because I have been giving over 10% of my income for about the past 35 years.

I've also received extreme blessings long before I knew they were coming as a result of my obedience. The blessings occurred long before I ever heard the story of Achen and Ai. I now considered my "First Fruits" obligation being complete. Nobody told me to do it. Nobody nagged at me to do it. I just did it because I knew it was the right thing to do along with a deep-seated fear of what will happen to me if I disobey. I have always believed violations of God's instructions will bring His anger.

I have church-going friends who have earnings higher than mine. In a round-about-way they have indicated to me that they do not give 10% or more. I notice these people struggle and are unhappy. They are irritable and restless. It seems to stem from economic insecurity, yet they are high income folks. Some are of very high income. They seem to have continual financial discontentment along with other serious problems of life. **Could these problems and ill feelings be the curse brought on by God** for violation of his covenant of First Fruits? It sure looks that way to me. What do you think?

Would I rather have 90% of my income blessed or 100% cursed? Some will ask where in the Bible does it say one will be cursed if they do not return 10% to God of all that comes to them? It's Malachi 3:9 plain as day!

Like Achen, will God have me killed and my body burned if I violate the covenant of First Fruits and/or do not return to God the 10% that has always belonged to Him? Will I be able to go to heaven if I have a red ink tithe? Can I go to heaven if I'm cursed? What about the time frame behind us? Would we be expected to somehow make up the amount we previously owed? No! I'm taught that our tithe obligation starts the day we repent of the sin of not tithing. It seems we are obligated from that day forward. What if I tithe for a few months and then skip a couple months and then start tithing again. Will I go to hell for skipping? That specific scenario is addressed in the King James translation but it's a hard ball batch of words. I'll short-cut the viewpoint from a number of scholars I have consulted. If you or I or any Christian skips the return of the tithe or part of the tithe, after making a pledge, then God will add a 20% penalty to the amount that you need to return. It's not 20% a year but a flat 20%. You may ask: Where is that in the bible? It's **Leviticus 27-31** as follows: **And if a man will at all redeem aught of his tithes, he shall add thereto the fifth part thereof.** (KJV) Wow! I'm going to obey for sure and have been doing so for about 35 years now. Many years before I ever read Leviticus 27-31, I obeyed. I'm sure glad I did. It's a frightening thing to violate His covenants. What's the solution to avoid the fear and fright? **Obey ! !**

He left the 99 to rescue me !

NOTES

CHAPTER 7

ANNA GIVES $1,000,000

My wife and I had a nice relation with a very rich couple. I will not mention them by name and will re-name the wife Anna. She grew up as the daughter of an ultra-rich oil billionaire from Lubbock Texas. They even made a movie about her daddy. Anna and her husband admired my wife because of her obvious and excellent relationship with the God of The Holy Trinity. I think maybe the reason they perhaps admired me was that they had learned of my extensive self-funded nationwide ministry activities.

Anna developed difficulties during her mid-life years, which led to severe depressions. The family tried to get help for her through psychiatrists. They prescribed drugs that seemed to make things worse. Anna had been a believer in God the Father, The Lord Jesus and The Holy Spirit, but had not been extremely active in church. Perhaps partially because of my Wife's Christian witness toward Anna, she became more active in seeking help from God. She began to tithe and as we learned later, indications were that she made a $1,000,000 gift/offering to her local church. So please ponder this question. Did God open the windows of heaven and pour out blessings to Anna in the form of additional money based on the scriptures of Malachi 3: 8-10? We suspect God did not. Anna did not need more money. She had tons of it. Blessings came to her in another form although I don't think she figured it out until months later. Her blessings seemed to come in another form. Her disposition seemed to slowly change and change drastically. We could see peace and contentment on her face. She seemed to be more and more at home with Jesus as we would visit with her. It did not take long, and she knew very well what was happening to her. As she continued to tithe and I assume make offerings, blessings began to overtake her in a wonderful way. Peace, love and contentment began to radiate from her face. The blessings were coming in abundance and in a form that was much more valuable to her than money. How much is joy unspeakable and peace that passes all understanding worth? How much is deliverance from black depressions worth?

So to the Gentile fat cats and the Jewish fat cats I ask: Can you buy your way out of a difficult life? Of course not. But what will happen if you make a pledge and keep the pledge to The God of our fathers and provide 10% of your upcoming income and to make offerings above the 10% to the Church of The God of Abraham Isaac and Jacob and to other New Testament or Old Testament (Tanakh) Bible based ministries, whether Christian, Messianic or Jewish? What do you think will happen? Probably the same thing that happened to sweet Anna. Giving softens the heart making it easier to receive deliverance from difficulties. Please remember, Malachi was written to a Jewish Congregation and also applies to Christians.

The tithe opens the windows of heaven. The offerings prompt the blessings to flow which are more valuable than gold, silver, cash, stocks, money market certificates, cattle, land or jewels. Far more valuable. More than Anna could contain? Yes, for sure! That's what she said, not me. If you believe there is a God, take Him up on his instructions, write the check and say to Him, **I'm putting You to the test** (prove Me now says the Lord of Hosts based on Malachi 3:10). **You are going to like** joy unspeakable and peace that passes all understanding. Then when or if we get to Heaven, we can talk to Anna about it. **What a day that will be** when our Messiah/Savior we shall see.

He left the 99 to rescue me !

CHAPTER 8

AN ACCOUNT IN HEAVEN

Christians may be surprised to learn that they have an account in Heaven. You may ask: Why would I need an account in heaven? You probably will not need the account once you get to heaven. While the account is in heaven during this mortal life, the account is for use now, while we are on this earth, not once you get to heaven. The account just happens to be located in heaven and is for usage now, today if needed.

Let's take a closer look at this occurrence. I have had a bank account here on earth since my teenage years. I've made deposits and withdraws on a regular basis as needed. The Apostle Paul writes a letter of Christian instructions to a Synagogue located in the town of Philippi. This mixed Jewish and

Gentile Congregation is advised about the fruit that should abound to their account. When I read it, I wondered, what account? Is Paul writing about their account in heaven? This is the clearest in the King James translation in Philippians 4:17. Obviously the Christians in Philippi have and account in heaven so can we conclude that we too have an account in heaven? Yes of course! So how do I make a deposit in my account in heaven? By doing good deeds that's how. We can do far more effective good deeds with a fat wallet than can be done with no money, a smile and a frothy emotional appeal. Which would do a person the most good if they were hungry? Some food purchased by us as an act of charity or a sugared up whining type greeting of sympathy. Charitable acts from cash could be the reason God wants us to prosper, so we can support ministries in His name.

Those who do not produce fruit are of little to no use to The Kingdom. The Bible does not say they will not be there, it just indicates they are of little to no use. When a person lives from payday to payday on barely get along, and drives a near junk dirty car, how attractive do you think they might be to an evangelical effort? The non-believers are not going to want to be a part of a religion that produces middle to low-income trashy witnesses. When I show up in neat clean attractive clothes, in a near new shiny car, and provide rent money for a single mom who is nearly 7 months pregnant and is about to be evicted, what do you think she is going to say after she stops crying tears of gratitude? Usually those of like situations ask ---- what church are you with? When I tell them, do you think we will have any trouble getting her to attend once her life smooths out? She will be eager and feel privileged to attend. That's what a prosperous income can produce. God wants you to have it. He wants you in the shiny new car, well dressed and say, what I'm privileged to give to you I give it in the name of the King of Kings who is Jesus and wants above all things for you also to prosper, even as your soul prospers. Sound familiar? (see III John 2)

How much was laid up in my account in heaven after doing a deed like that for the young mother. How much would be in my heavenly account if I continued those type activities for another 40 to 50 years? You will say, that's easy for you, because you are a fat cat. I wasn't when I came to Jesus in 1976. I was broke, hungover, angry, bitter, hostile and heavy in debt. But not for long, because one of the first things I did was to stop playing poker, stop drinking alcohol and started working hard on the job. Next, I repented of my non-tithing. Then I started **returning the 10%** from my income of that day forward. The tithe has belonged to Jesus all along. That 10% never has been mine. All the tithes of ever person on earth have always belonged to Jesus. It just crossed our palm, that's all. Maybe He wants to see what we will do with that which He provides. Supporting the causes of our Lovely Lord Jesus can become fun. It's even more fun when the windows of heaven open based on the **return of the tithe** and then even more fun as the **blessing flow out** as a result of the offerings, the amount above the 10%. The windows were popped opened by the **return of the tithe.** The **blessing began to flow** as a result of the offerings.

How do we make withdraws from our account in heaven? Ask for it!

He left the 99 to rescue me !

NOTES

CHAPTER 9

AN APPRECIATION RESPONSE

In church we often hear the words, tithes and offerings. If you ask the preacher the difference between the two, you can tell they usually don't know. So, I looked up the words in the dictionary. The Standard Dictionary and a Bible Dictionary. (A Bible Dictionary is one where the only words in this dictionary are the words that are in the bible.) No other words are included. The word tithe is defined as 10%. An offering is that which is offered for usage. It does not include a specific percentage. Gifts are also mixed into the church vocabulary. A gift is that which is provided out of love, affection or concern with no expectation of getting it back. An offering is different. Consider the following example.

One evening as we were driving home from a meeting, I noticed my neighbor Allen working in his garage. He had his Volkswagen on jack stands with the engine disassembled on the garage floor. I realized it would take him nearly all night to get that car running in order for him to get to work in the morning. I knew he had only one car. If he did not get the car fixed, he would have to lie and call in sick and perhaps get himself in trouble on the job or get fired. I had an idea. I walked up to his garage and told him I would put my pickup truck in our driveway, put the key under the floor mat and if he did not get his car fixed, he could use my truck and not have to miss work. I **offered** Allen the use of my pickup truck so that he would not have to work all night and perhaps not make it to work. It was an **"offering."** It was not a gift. I fully expected to get it back. I **offered** it to him for his usage fully expecting to **get my "offering" back.** I did not tell him to keep it. It was not a gift. I provided an **"offering"** to Allen. There were no strings attached. No stipulations. No requirements needed in order for him to accept. While there were no strings attached, I did expect some sort of an **appreciation response.** A simple thank you would be fine but nothing more. One thing was for sure. **I fully expected to get my truck back.** I did not tell him **it is a gift and you can keep it.** I expected for it to be returned to me.

And so it is with my **offerings to God.** I fully expect to get it back in one form or another along with a simple **appreciation response.**

You may scoff at such a belief and viewpoint, but you have not seen my financial statement or witnessed the blessings that come my way time after time for these past 45 years. They are so numerous I don't even tell anybody about them anymore because I don't want to listen to them tell me how lucky I am. I'm not lucky because luck does not exist. The wonderful blessings I receive come from God not from luck. When He provides an appreciation response it's usually easy to figure out what's happening. It **comes from offerings** and it comes right out of the windows of heaven! He can provide whatever type and size of appreciation response He so decides, and He does so time after time. **Not so with those who do not tithe.** Please remember now the tithe only opens the windows of heaven and the **offerings** bring the pouring out of blessings. It seems those **blessings far exceed the offerings.** Why should He provide for us blessings if we have not even **returned to Him** that which already belongs to Him (the tithe) all along. The pecking order seems essential.

He left the 99 to rescue me !

CHAPTER 10

BIBLICAL LAWS

At the beginning of my bible seeking experience, I had incorrect definitions of various words used. The word "law" was one of them. I thought that when the word "law" was used it was referring to the 10 Commandments and other various commands. That's correct in some areas but there is more than one bible definition of the word law. One other definition is; **something is absolutely positively going to happen.** Such as; it's law that the sun comes up in the east, or if you fall out of a tree, it's law that you are absolutely positively going to go down based on the "law of gravity." And so it is with all of **God's Biblical Laws.** There really is a **Biblical Law of Prosperity.** God's laws are in concrete so to speak. They are not going to change whether we believe them or do not believe them. You can scoff at us who believe **The Law of Biblical Prosperity** but that's not going to stop God from doing what He says toward those of us who implement His **Law of Biblical Prosperity** with the **predominant objective** of being able to acquire more funding to promote **His various ministries** around the world! It's my belief that God is **not** going to prosper me for the **single purpose** of buying another Corvette, an ultra-fancy house along with my first Lear jet. He want's me to have the finer things in life but that should not be my **predominant objective,** nor should it be my **predominant expenditure.** To support those who bring about the elimination of pain and suffering comes first. Especially among the wonderful Jewish people who have been horribly discriminated against through history like no others. Gee, I wonder if Luke 6:38 might apply to such a viewpoint? ----- Which says: **"Give and it shall be given unto you; good measure, pressed down, shaken together and running over will men give unto your**

bosom." I have had men hand me a big fat check from a business deal and point the envelope that contained the check right toward to middle of my chest. Is that what God is talking about in Luke 6:38 when He says thru Luke, "**shall men give unto your bosom.**" Isn't the middle of my chest the same as my bosom? It sure looks to me like that is what Luke is describing. What do you think? That was my thought the first time it happened. Then over the years it has happened time and time again. Then the thought comes: **Hello envelope, It's great to see you again!**

First, I return the tithe of every dime that comes my way, which opened the windows of heaven. The windows were opened but I still had a near empty wallet. Open windows won't fill a wallet. We need something to start the flow of blessings out through those opened windows. Then the gifts and offerings were made, which **starts the flow of the pouring out of blessings!** The blessings don't start by returning the tithe, which already belongs to God, the blessing **start**

from offerings and gifts, which is the amount above the tithe. This entire chapter is the way it's interpreted by this writer. How do you see this entire chapter? What's your experience?

He left the 99 to rescue me !

CHAPTER 11

WHERE TO TITHE

Most church members have heard preachers quote Malachi 3: 8-10 when it comes time to perk up a sagging church budget, or during an annual fundraising effort. It's usually not a fun message. But if you first consider and implement a financial disbursement like God is instructing and like I'm trying to relay, then it becomes a lot of fun ! Who would not enjoy prosperity? It does not come overnight but it will come. It is law. Just like the sun comes up in the east. It is law! As has been outlined numerous times in this volume, the requirement is to **return the Tithe** and to **provide offerings.** Not just tithes but also offerings and gifts. Those are two different things. The tithe is 10% and the offerings and gifts are the amount over 10%.

Most preachers will say "bring all the tithe into the storehouse" meaning bring all into that specific church. I was reading Deuteronomy and bumped into Chapter 26:12-13. it says:

Each third year you must offer a special tithe of your crops. In this year of special tithe, you must give your tithes to the Levites, sojourners, fatherless, and widows. Then you must declare in the presence of the Lord your God, I have taken the sacred gift from my house and given it to the Levites, sojourners, fatherless and widows, just as you have commanded me. I have not forgotten any of your commands.

Most of us have similar difficulty unraveling this scripture just like Malachi 3:8-10. I'll address this in the form of a testimony from a fellow who has successfully implemented God's Biblical Laws of Prosperity. Me! It's my story and needs no editing. It's very accurate.

Deuteronomy tells us of crops to be given. I don't have any crops, I'm a former businessman and now a retired fat cat living on a juicy retirement income. So, I decided my retirement income is my crop and I'm going to give it. Next, I asked myself, who are the Levites in my life today? So, I got out my dictionaries and considered all the various definitions and decided it was the clergy and those who assist the clergy. It's the church workers, which includes the most important worker of the entire staff, the janitor. If the preacher was gone for a couple of months and then the janitor was gone for a couple of months, which one do you think would be missed the most? Enough said! Therefore, I placed some of God's tithe and my gifts and offerings to the local church so that they may make payroll for the preacher, his staff and the most important person there, the janitor!

The next category mentioned in Deuteronomy 26:12 is sojourners. Who and what is a sojourner in my life today? My dictionaries indicate that it's people who are moving from one local to another. I discovered a ministry that helps elderly Jewish people to migrate from areas of poverty back to their homeland of Israel. They became one of my financial targets and I sent them a nice batch of bucks.

I thought about all the millions of immigrants coming across our southern border illegally. Should we help these sojourners who are breaking our laws as they enter America? I wouldn't think so. Then the thought came to me about the children of these immigrants who get separated from their parents for one reason or another. I located a ministry in south Texas that explained how they are helping hundreds and hundreds of them. It's a very sad story. I verified what I had learned and decided these were child sojourners and I supported this children's ministry in a healthy way.

The next category is the fatherless. That would include the children of single mothers. I had to be careful here, so I went to the church secretary and asked if the church had any single moms who were struggling financially. She indicated she knew of two. I told her not to give me their names but to forward a gift to them. I went to the bank and got $1000 cash, took it to the church secretary and asked her to give $500 in cash directly to the moms but don't tell me who they are or tell them who I am. You have to play it safe when you are a geezer like me. We cannot be giving young ladies cash, or we could get put in jail just based on the mountain of innuendo that would develop.

I found a ministry that helps the fatherless through single moms. It is a live-in facility for young ladies who are pregnant and homeless and do not want to abort the child. Ladies, could you imagine what it would be like to be about 17 years old and 7 or 8 months pregnant, homeless and sleeping in the back seat of a car that had run out of gas. She was in the back seat covered up under her belongings to keep warm. She told of how she had been praying nearly all night to God begging Him not to allow her baby to have a life like she had. A highway patrolman tapped on the window with a flashlight, figured out the situation and took her to the local Sheriff's office. The lady dispatcher there **just happened to be a devout Christian.** She got some food into the young girl and made arrangements with some of her church lady friends who took control of the situation and arranged for her to be admitted into the Home for young girls who refuse to abort. That home for girls has for years been heavy on God's tithe list managed by me, along with my gifts and offerings. I don't know how many **tens of thousands of dollars I have given over the years to those type homes.**

The next category is widows. Back to the church secretary. Every Sunday one very elderly widow greeted my wife and I with extreme kindness and graciousness, along with dozens of other members. I later asked the church secretary about her financial condition and was told it was thin and very thin. Back to the bank for another $1000 in cash and then had the church secretary slip all of it to her and not to tell her who gave it.

Our local City Rescue Mission has a number of widows housed who are homeless. You guessed it, my bucks went their way.

That takes care of the four places where I'm instructed to place God's tithe and my offerings and gifts, once each three years. Now what about the other two years? I don't know. I don't have a clue exactly what to do so I just make sure that 12%, sometimes 15%, sometimes 20% and sometimes way over 20%, gets to the four categories of Deuteronomy 26:12-13. People will say it's easy for you fat cats because you have got so much money. Not so in my case. When I came to Jesus. I was broke and deep in debt. I had been planning bankruptcy and knew the creditors and lawyers would get all that was on hand, so I gave it to Church and surprisingly a blessing came my way. Because of that blessing which I believe came from God, I was able to avoid bankruptcy. I heard the Prosperity message preached on Christian T V and believed it, so I participated by returning God's tithe to Him and providing some offerings and gifts.

Today I'm doing rather well. I give God the credit.

All the money on earth belongs to God. That which I have acquired and control, does not belong to me. It comes through me but not from me. It comes from God.

My extreme prosperity started when I believed the T V preacher who obviously presented it to me correctly. I obviously implemented it correctly. Any person can do the same. All it takes is His tithe and your offerings and gifts.

God tells me of four different places to put God's tithe and my offerings and gifts and to do so once each three years. The four targets are: Levites, sojourners, fatherless, and widows. What am I supposed to do the other 2 years? I don't know for sure. I try to focus a little more on one of the specific areas where there seems to be more of a need at that particular time. It varies.

He left the 99 to rescue me !

CHAPTER 12

PETERS FAITH AND MONEY

I had a preacher buddy who liked to go fishing with me. He was more experienced than I was so he usually caught more fish. At one outing we were trout fishing. For nearly an hour we had caught nothing. My friend moved to a spot where a stream trickled into the lake, which contained more oxygen than the rest of the lake water. Small bubbles verified this. The bubbles near the shoreline also indicate a higher oxygen content. Fish like oxygen, they have to have it. If I wanted to catch fish then I had to fish where the fish are, not where they aren't. There are hardly any fish out in the deep because there is far less oxygen in the deep.

Jesus' disciples were professional fisherman in Galilee. The amount of money in their pockets depended upon their fishing skills. As a result of financial need, no doubt they knew a lot about fishing. I was in Israel where the Jordan River aggressively flows downward from the mountains. There are four or more fisherman mentioned in Luke 5: 1-11. Where were these guys fishing when Jesus instructs them to launch out into the deep and let down your nets? They were near the mouth of the Jordan River where the oxygen content of the water was high. No doubt they had often fished this area with good success because of the high oxygen content in the water and the fish being attracted to that area of high oxygen content. But Jesus tells them to launch out into the deep and let down your nets. Peter's past experience tells him there are no fish out in the deep that we want to catch. Those out in the deep are scarce and are bottom feeders, like catfish. This type fish were forbidden as food at that time per the instructions of God to Moses. The fish that are near the shore and near the mouth of the Jordan River where the oxygen content of the water is high, are the type that are acceptable and edible. Peter tells Jesus that we have fished all night and caught nothing. His mind set had to be; a Rabbi wants to tell us professional fisherman how and where to fish ! But nevertheless, I'll obey and go out and fish the deep, where we have never had good success, and we will do so just because you are the Lord and you say so. To the shock of these fisherman, they caught so many edible fish that the nets started breaking.

I was in a grocery store in Tiberius, which is located on the west side of the Sea of Galilee, buying some snack foods. I noticed some fillets of Saint Peters fish (talipia) on display and the prices. Wow! The price was about 3 or 4 times what we pay in America for the same type fish. Food is extremely expensive in that part of the world. Per the average budget it was a great deal more expensive 2000 years ago. The scholars teach that families had to toil hard all week long just to be able to pay for food. Food was a very valuable commodity then and now. The scriptures tell us that Peter and his crew filled two boat loads full of fish. So full they were nearly ready to sink. How much money would two full boat loads of fish bring on the market at that time? I did some rough calculations from the "Tables of Weights and Measures and Coins" from my Ryrie Study Bible. My conversion efforts were rough but in a general way I was able to come up with about $250,000 worth of fish, in today's money, coming from two fishing boats the size of those used in Jesus' day. The two boats were so full of fish they nearly sank. **If we obey Jesus' instruction, prosperity often follows,** whether we are expecting it or not. **Sometimes big prosperity.** Peter, James and John, the sons of Zebedee, were partners in the commercial fishing business. They were very wealthy to begin with. You had to be wealthy to be able to own commercial fishing boats. They became a great deal more wealthy after the whopper catch brought on by the miracle of Jesus' instructions to launch out into the deep and let down your nets where they had never caught any large volume of fish before.

The traditional image of Jesus and those who followed Him as being poor just seems and is all wrong as I study my Bible. **His followers were wealthy and prosperous,** and they became more so as they obeyed Jesus the day they let down there nets into the deep. I am convinced that **God does not want his children to be poor.** Do you want your children to be poor? Does God want his children to be on **average to below average income?** Do you want your children to be on average to below average income? Does God want his children to **live on "barely get along"?** Do you want your children to live on barely get along?

May we be blessed by The God Of The Holy Trinity with financial prosperity as we obey and fish. If we don't obey there may not be an overflowing boatload. If we don't go fishing, there won't be an overflowing boat load for sure. To obey brings financial prosperity and much more. It brings a trip to the City of Gold.

He left the 99 to rescue me !

NOTES

CHAPTER 13

BY THE SHED BLOOD

OR BY GRACE?

God Our Father, The Lord Jesus, who is The Only Christ, The Only Messiah Of Israel, The Only Savior Of The World, along with The Comforting Holy Spirit can bless **whoever** They want to, **whenever** They want to and with **whatever type** and **quantity** of blessings They so decide. Malachi 3:8-10 does make it easier for us. I'm very grateful for such instructions. God has packaged this specific procedure for us and outlined it in Malachi 3:8-10. Will The God of the Holy Trinity bless those in a **cult?** I don't know, you'll have to ask God not me, but if He does, I would not think it would be to the point that is mentioned in Malachi 3:10 where the blessings are so abundant that the recipient cannot contain it all. One scholar suggests the translation should perhaps read "so much that the recipient will not know what to do with all of it," or where to place it all. That is what has happened to this writer. I don't know for sure where to put all the financial blessings that are coming to me, but I am making some various ministries real happy.

People who are caught up in a **cult** usually do not know they are in a **cult**. A good definition of a **cult** is; any gathering that seeks spiritual matters but excludes any one of the three entities of the Holy Trinity as mentioned at the beginning of this chapter.

Many clergy today know that drastic changes are occurring in today's Churches. Many are becoming the apostate church mentioned as an occurrence that takes place just before the rapture of the true Christians. My wife and I had a friendship with a nationally known preacher who was excellent in so many ways. He said that in his early career he preached at church's where He did not think one person there was going to heaven. That was not a judgment, it was an opinion. The lack of fruit being produced prompted his conclusion.

The point I'm trying to make is: It seems likely that not all **liberal** church going persons, **Laodiceans, pseudo** christians and church going **cult** worshipers are not going to have as much success with Malachi 3:8-10 as devout Bible obedient Christians. Acting upon and believing false teachings might just be a real handicap toward receiving blessings. The following concerns **hyper grace teachings** which might be one of dozens of examples.

It is fashionable these days for clergy to preach on grace. Preached, preached and over preached are the messages of grace. He gave us the **plan** of salvation by his grace, not the implementation of the **plan**. One scholar I'm familiar with calls it hyper grace teaching. The correct view is that He gave us the **plan** of salvation by His grace, not the implementation of the **plan**. The scripture incorrectly used by hyper grace teachers is Ephesians Chapter 2, verse 8. From an easy to understand paraphrase: *For by grace you are saved through faith and not of yourselves, it is the gift of God.* Chapter 1 comes before Chapter 2. Chapter 1 indicates we are **saved by the shed blood.** So which is it? By the **shed blood** in Chapter 1 or **by grace** in Chapter 2 ? Perhaps the grace teachers ought to read Chapter 1 before they quote Chapter 2. This is the reason why numbers are put in front of each chapter. The number 1 comes before number 2 !!! We are **saved by the shed blood,** in Chapter 1 not by grace as it's presented by the hyper grace teachers. Using the easy to understand paraphrase we can discover the word **"plan"** being used in four different places in Chapter 1. From Chapter 1, verse 5.... *from his unchanging plan....* and in verse 9.... *God's secret plan....* and again in verse 9.... *It is a plan centered on The Christ.....* and again in verse 10..... *And this is His plan....*

What **plan**? What **plan** is God inspiring the Apostle Paul to describe to us? The **plan** that includes the shed blood unto salvation that's what!!! It's the **plan** He gave us **by His**

grace, not the implementation of it. To implement the **plan** that He gave us **by His grace**, we need to take a look at what Paul is telling the Church in Rome as he writes to them. From the letter of Romans 10:9 it is clearly suggested we are going to have to do some confessing from our mouth. That's the same as telling others. We are going to have to speak to others of Jesus Christ as The Lord of our life. As we proceed, we are going to have to understand the definition of the word **"Lord."** To make Jesus The **Lord** of my life is similar to making Jesus The **Boss** of my life. Next, we need to repent. What does it mean? It means to turn from the way we have been living, to try to change and live by God's instructions as best we can, He, being our helper. Next, we are going to have to do some believing in our **heart.** To believe within our heart means it's deep within us. It's part of us. Memorization of scripture helps to believe deep within our heart. Believing what? That Jesus was raised from the dead!

Let's recap this: We must tell others. We must make Him our Lord. We must change,

He, being our helper. We must believe in our heart that Jesus was raised from the dead. This is how we implement the **plan** that He gave us **by His grace.** He did not have to give us this **plan.** He gave us the **plan** by His grace. It's the **plan** He gave us by His grace, not the implementation of it!

What does this have to do with The Biblical Laws Of Prosperity? Perhaps unsaved **liberal** church goers, **Ladodiceans, pseudo** christians and church going **cult** worshipers suffer from blessings blockage. What do you think? Are there dozens of incorrect doctrines that cause blessings blockage? Is Malachi 3: 8-10 for devout Christians only. I don't know all the answers. Ask God, not me !

He left the 99 to rescue me !

CHAPTER 14

DON'T BURY IT IN THE GROUND

Most of us Christians have heard over and over the Bible parable of the men being given talents by their master. A talent is an old English word that means "a monetary unit" The parable appears in Matthew 25: 14-30. Bible students will agree that a talent is a large amount of money if they will use a dictionary. Exactly how much money brings a big debate but several scholars say one talent could be worth about $1,000,000 in today's money. Therefore, I'll use that number so our mathematics will be easy to follow. I'll also skip the details of the parable hoping you will read it for yourself. A shortened version of the parable indicates one servant was given five talents or $5,000,000. Another servant was given two talents or

$2,000,000. The third was given one talent or $1,000,000. The first servant invested the money and doubled the $5,000,000 to $10,000,000 and gave the money to his Master which pleased Him. The second doubled his $2,000,000 to $4,000,000 and gave it to his Master which pleased Him. The third servant **buried the $1,000,000 in the ground** and when the Master returned he give him back the $1,000,000 which angered the Master greatly to the point that He called him a worthless servant and cast him into outer darkness which most say is the same as destroying his body and his soul !

Perhaps we should all read this parable carefully, several times and after pondering it please join me in asking our self, how does this apply to me in my life today?

If the Master in the parable represents God, and I think it does, He gives these three servants far far in excess of what they need to survive. He gives them a huge surplus. Therefore, I will conclude, right or wrong, that the parable will apply to those who have far far more money than is needed to survive.

Those with high income, should **put the excess big money to work** with the result being to bring increase and pleasure to the Master, not the income of your average Joe's.

I'm not comfortable with this viewpoint but I cannot come up with a different viewpoint. According to my dictionary a parable is a **comparison story** to bring about a religious principal or moral attitude. Since a parable is a comparison story, we have to be able to compare it to something and someone of every day life. Therefore, I'll move forward with this view and consider that the parable probably does not apply to your average Joe, or the average family budget but does apply to the rich and the ultra-rich fat cats. I will use as an example, for comparison, a man we shall call Bob. He is not a character of fiction. He is in the category of the rich. It appears to me that the rich are the only ones the parable applies to. Who else could it be compared to? Your average Joe is not going to have somebody hand him $5,000,000 to invest. It's directed to those with money far in excess of what is needed and who know how to manage it.

As an American, Bob's total assets are big, but not all that big compared to many in the circles within which he lives, but he is one of the rich, just not the ultra-rich. But on the other hand, when compared to all people in the world today, and yesterday, he would be in at least, the upper 1/10th of one percent of all population. Bob has a retirement income which he can live on for the rest of his life without any worry. He cannot draw on the principal of the retirement income as it comes from a third party. Bob's elderly wife is bed-ridden and house-bound with no need of an inheritance. He had only one child and she is married to a successful businessman with no need for an inheritance. Same with the only two grandchildren. Bob has a rather large saving account within a bank. He also has C D's and other valuables. All had been tithed on. **Figuratively it's all buried within the bank vault.** The money just sits there drawing an **inconsequential** very low rate of return which only accumulates in that bank vault. It's like **it's all inactive as it's buried inside the bank vault.** In Bob's case, **what's the difference of the money being buried in a bank vault or in the ground?** Like the third man in the Bible parable who **buried $1,000,000 in the ground, Bob buried it in the bank vault.** What's the difference? **None!** It appears there is no difference. In Bob's case the money was not being put to use to further the advancement of the harvesting of souls for God. Because he has **not** put it into usage toward that which he can return to God (his Master), will Bob be cast into outer darkness which indicates he and his soul will be destroyed **like the third man in the parable**? Is Bob like the third man in the parable? He did not know, but he wondered! This exact view troubled Bob, so he started to disperse the surplus monies. He started giving to one responsible ministry after another. To the various T V ministries, to orphanages, to the fatherless, to numerous Churches, directly to needy widows, to Christian relief ministries, to homes for pregnant girls who refused to abort, to

Christian schools and universities, to radio ministries, to prison ministries, to ministries aimed at our military, to Christian sponsored homeless shelters, ministries that help the people of Israel, to ministries that help the poverty stricken Jews in Israel, and **on and on.** To most of these he gave $1000 at a time and to some $5000 increments. Bob put only a small dent in the buried bank money before he even dumped 1/4th of it. Then something happened. Unknowingly based on God's Holy Word in Malachi 3: 8-10, financial blessings started pouring out in abundance thru those opened windows of heaven again. Blessings had poured out in years past. That's where the savings came from to begin with. Bob was already rich, but he acquired a huge windfall from those opened windows again while he was dispersing the tithed savings. The windfall was near $1,000,000, in today's money, prompted by a dormant occurrence in Bob's life of nearly 60 years ago. **What an incredible miracle!** It was like the **first** man in the parable who received the $1,000,000 from the **third man** due to his lack of investment. Now Bob has more money to disperse than before.

Parables get complicated. It is the responsibility of each believer to study and pray about the amount which is **buried in the bank**. Let's somewhat recap the parable. The first two servants returned to the master the principal and the gain. So how do I return the principal and the gain? Who do I make the check out to? In Chapter 11 of this writing, we consider the Levitcs, sojourners, fatherless and widows **once each three years.** Chapter 11 gives us several practical examples and I'm sure you could come up with more. What about the other two years? Bob's criteria was that the recipient must be distinctively Christian and favorably and frequently use the name of Jesus (or **Yeshua** which is His name in His own Hebrew language). If the primary subjects they teach are predominantly Old Testament, used as **a form of flock pacification**, and frequently excluded the New Testament parables and other teachings of Jesus then Bob puts them at the bottom of the list.

Other ways to give back to God are made clear in Matthew 25:35-46, which addresses the least of these of society. It reads like a ministry check list. When I give to the **least of these,** it's the same as giving to the Lord Jesus himself. If I do not give to the least of these the response from Jesus is rather harsh. It does not sound like Heaven to me.

He left the 99 to rescue me !

CHAPTER 15

UNFRUITFUL FIG TREE

By returning God's tithe to Him which has often been mentioned in this volume, by doing so I can only conclude that such return is not impressive to God. After all, it's always been His anyway. Perhaps it's some sort of an obedience and trust test. My gifts and offerings to the poor and to the suffering seem to be different than the return of the tithe. Perhaps such an effort will give God a grin. I hope so. Once we start even the slightest of such activity, it changes us. It does not take long for an overwhelming desire to eliminate suffering one way or another. My rule is that if it is for the causes of Jesus and the ministry has His name or title attached and is distinctively Christian then that's all I need to know, I'll support it. When doing so it's easy to figure out that I'm bearing fruit. Some of the readers of this writing have done the same. To those who are on the fence and perhaps thinking of placing some gift and offering money, big or small, I hope they do so and hopefully they will quickly acquire the peace and contentment that comes along with the financial blessings. Often times the joy unspeakable and peace that passes all understanding is worth more than the financial returns of Malachi 3:8-10.

With some of the financial blessings God had returned to me, I took a trip to Israel. I spent 10 days and nights in a Hotel located on the west side of the Sea of Galilee. I took a new easy to read New Living Bible. Every day I would walk along the Sea of Galilee from Capernaum toward where Jesus taught the Sermon On The Mount. I was sitting on a large smooth rock at the water's edge reading from my bible. Probably the same rock Jesus had sat on, and I stumbled onto a very interesting scripture. It was Mark 4: 33. I'll paraphrase what it said. *In his public ministry*

He (Jesus) *taught only with the parables.* The parable of the unfruitful fig tree had been my favorite for years. Probably because I had been doing what it tells us that we had better do or else! I had been doing it for several years before I ever read the parable, I had been doing so and doing a lot of what it says. I had been bearing fruit and lots of it. It is such a hardball parable. You can interpret it however you decide but to me, the comparison story clearly indicates it's necessary for us to bear fruit or God will cut us down. His ax is poised. (Matthew 7:19) How can that be compared to anything other than death and destruction for the unfruitful? Scary isn't it? That's why I have done so much. I am not scared now. Funny how that works.

The following is from Luke 13: 6-9 from this author's paraphrase.

A certain man had a fig tree that he had planted in his vineyard. He came looking for fruit on it and didn't find any. He said to the vineyard keeper: For three years I have come looking for fruit on this fig tree without finding any. Cut it down! Why should it be using up the ground? And the vineyard keeper answered and said to him, let it alone, sir, this year too until I dig around it and put in fertilizer; and if it bears fruit next year fine; but if not cut it down.

A good Bible definition of the word parable is: a comparison story dealing with ordinary life from which a moral message or religious truth is taught.

Who is who in the parable of Luke 13:6-9? Who is being compared to who, and what is being compared to what? In verse 6, one of the things we can notice is that he says a fig tree is growing in a vineyard. Isn't a vineyard where they grow grapes? What is a fig tree doing growing in the middle of a bunch of grape vines? Wouldn't that be something like a watermelon growing in the middle of a wheat field? Perhaps he wants us to know there is more than one type of fruit that needs to be produced and that type is not always the same type the vast majority around us is producing. In verse 7 we see a character enter the scene; **the vine dresser.** The job of the vine dresser would be to look after the wellbeing of these fruit bearing plants. Is Jesus the vine dresser in this parable? I think he is. Are you and I a fig tree? Looks like it to me. Is God our Father the owner of the vineyard? I believe so.

Continuing in verse 7, we see the owner of the vineyard give a specific time period of three years, in which he has waited for fruit to grow. Trees should bear fruit every year. It's not hard for a tree to bear fruit, because that's the natural thing for it to do. It's unnatural for it not to bear fruit. Something is stopping it. Jesus, being the vine dresser jumps right into the picture. He makes arrangements for it to be saved and he acquires more time on behalf of the tree, another year, (a total of four years) in the hopes that it might be spared from being cut down. As he arranges an extra year's reprieve for the tree, he then promises to nourish it and help it grow toward a healthy condition. He is doing all of this for the tree without the tree requesting it and without the tree knowing anything about it. Then at the end of this additional year for it to bear fruit, a total of four years in the parable, he says that if no fruit; then thou shall cut it down!

I have experienced this parable being played out with the observation of death (being cut down) occurring right in front of my nose and have witnessed it numerous times. Having done an enormous amount of ministry work toward those within the alcohol drug recovery movement, I listen to them talk and testify about how hard it is for those within this recovery activity to get over what they call the five-year hump. It seems that between years four and five of sobriety, things become extremely difficult. The thoughts of drink and drugs overpowers many. Most do not make it past the five-year period of being clean and sober. The vast majority of that movement relapse and die. A personal observation of mine was that those who do make it past four years and then over the five-year hump, are those who had been actively engaged in working with others. Helping others. Bearing fruit! I mentioned this to a church elder once. The only thing he did was to say --- very interesting. He did not make any indication whatsoever that he would like to help. I wondered if the **elder** was going to be cut down ! I also tried to encourage a **preacher** to help. He did the same as the elder. They seemed **to care less** about the former drunks, junkies, the poor, the suffering, the sick and crazy, let alone do anything about it. Is it appropriate to say; Woe unto them? I'm comfortable with this hardball parable. If you are disturbed by it, please think of some way to put some of your cash into an offering in order to bear fruit. It's not that hard. All it takes is just a little cash over the tithe as an offering. You will never miss it.

So what does this have to do with the Bible Laws Of Prosperity? It has everything to do with **our prosperity and our survival.** When we make financial offerings, the money comes back in increased amounts making it much easier to support more various activities that bring about the harvesting of souls to receive eternal life with Jesus, that where He is, there you, and hopefully me and others may be also! (John 14:3)

He left the 99 to rescue me !

CHAPTER 16

CONCLUSION

I know of a man who implemented the basic principles of God's prosperity promises and today has multiple billions of dollars. He and his wife had enough spare money that they built a multi-million-dollar Bible Museum on the Mall in Washington D C right near the Smithsonian Institute and did so totally with their own funding. When or if you visit the museum, you will learn a lot about the Bible. The beautiful building and the extremely valuable items displayed are evidence of the size and scope of the blessings being poured out through those opened windows, toward this couple. This couple that had the billions and built the place, did not start out rich. They started out with a part time sideline activity in his garage doing high quality custom picture framing in order to supplement his regular middle-income paycheck. He and his wife believed that they should tithe and did so. They also believed they should make offerings, give gifts and consider the poor and suffering. Blessings came pouring out of those opened windows and today they own nearly 1000 very large and profitable retail outlets in America.

For about 10 years I did the evening chapel service at our local City Rescue Mission. It's a facility to feed homeless people and keep them from sleeping on the streets. I arrived early in the evening before supper time to set up the music equipment. As I passed the large kitchen area I noticed a nice-looking lady, clean and neatly dressed with sweat on her brow working hard in the hot kitchen, stirring a huge pot of food. She had a look upon her face that indicated she was at peace, happy and contented. An appearance you do not often see at a homeless mission unless it's coming from one of us Christian volunteer workers. I stopped and went into the kitchen to offer a kind word of appreciation for her efforts. She received my kind words and did the same towards me. During that very short chit chat, suddenly I recognized her as I had been in her home for a social occasion months before. **It was the multi-billionaires wife working hard as a volunteer in the steaming hot kitchen!** Do you suppose that servitude like she provided had anything to do with acquiring the blessings her and her husband had received?

He left the 99 to rescue me !

NOTES

ITALICIZED WORDS
of the
KING JAMES TRANSLATION
of the Bible.

The original writings of what we would call The Old Testament were written in the Hebrew language. Most of the New Testament was written in the Greek language. Both were translated into the English language under the reign of King James of England. This translation was started in the early 1600's and completed in year 1611. The Nation of Israel did not exist at that time. The Jewish people had been scattered over the Mediterranean and other areas as a result of military activity against Israel. There were pockets of Jewish settlements in England. The Jewish scholars of these small segments of Jewish society where the ones who assisted the English translators to accomplish the completion of the English language bible.

In some areas of translation, we did not have an English word that was the equivalent to the Jewish or Greek word that was being translated. Many times there was no English word that meant the same as the Jewish word. Same with the Greek words. We did not have an English word that had the same meaning. Therefore, the translators inserted a word which they felt would suffice. When they inserted such a substitution word, those words are shown in italics. While reading a King James or New King James Bible, you will notice these numerous italicized words.

In Malachi 3: 10, there are 7 or 8 italicized words, depending on which KJV you're reading, which appear **in just this one verse.** No place in the Bible have I ever seen as many italicized words in just one verse. This means that 7 or 8 places in the Hebrew scriptures, in just one verse, the English translators had to scratch their heads and insert a word which they thought best fit the situation. The following is how the last part of verse 10 reads with the italicized words:

...and pour out for you *such* blessing that *there will* not *be room* enough *to receive it.*

Next let's look at it with the italicized words removed.

...and pour out for you blessing that not enough...

Surely this left the translators and us, with a whopper batch of confusion, which may effect the destiny of souls. But if we pray and study, I will assume you will come up with the same conclusion I did and that is: The fellows of year 1611 did a pretty good job of filling in the blanks, and I'm going to accept it and move forward with it as is.

He left the 99 to rescue me !

NOTES

MEAT:

DICTIONARY DEFINITIONS

The word "Meat' as it is being used in Malachi 8: 10 has brought enormous confusion. Preachers and Bible Teachers obviously do not make use of all the dictionaries available.

Before we consider the dictionaries, we need to realize the word "meat" is not referring to the flesh of animals used for human consumption. There was no refrigeration in those days and fresh meat would spoil, rot and stink. They would never bring such an item into a Synagogue. It is not referring to food other than the flesh of animals either. The Synagogue was not a cafeteria or food bank. One top scholar defined the word "meat" as financial supply. *From reference # 2964 of the Hebrew

Dictionary from the Strong's Exhaustive Concordance; **"meat."** It is defined as **spoil.**

Viewpoint: **Spoil;** that which is valuable and acquired, as the spoils of labor; also as in plunder from a battle. Example: Joshua 6:19

From an older Funk & Wagnall Dictionary, consider 3 definitions of the word **"meat"**

1: That which can be done with **ease**
2: That which can be enjoyed with **ease.**
3: That which is acquired with **ease.**

Viewpoint of #1: For those of us who regularly tithe and give offerings, it's done with **ease** when we realize blessings become far more valuable than the tithe and offerings combined. It's done with **ease.**

Viewpoint of #2: A church or synagogue can **enjoy** with **ease** tithes and offerings. Many providers like myself enjoy it too.

Viewpoint of #3: A church or synagogue can **acquire** tithes and offering with **easy** from well-developed believers. They don't even have to ask for it or nag about it.

From the New Websters Dictionary. One of several definitions:

Meat: Something **enjoyed.**

Viewpoint: I do **enjoy** it. I'm sure the clergy and staff **enjoy** receiving tithes and offerings.

**Storehouse: From the Hebrew Bible dictionary, reference #214; "treasury"

He left the 99 to rescue me !

NOTES

BIBLE TRANSLATIONS

The original manuscripts of the Old Testament were written in the Hebrew language. Most of the New Testament was originally written in the Greek language with some in Hebrew.

Bible translations, when complicated sometimes bring unbelief. Many Christians, including some of the top scholars, do not believe the prosperity message of the Bible. Often it is because they have not used dictionaries. Especially cross reference dictionaries which tie the English, Greek and Hebrew languages all together.

The Greek and Hebrew dictionaries have been converted into the English language. It's easy to understand. Hard to pronounce the words but easy to figure out the various definitions. It's unwise to argue the views generated with the use of dictionaries, especially, cross references Bible Dictionaries, which contain only the words used in the Bible.

The English translation of the Bible commonly used today was completed in England in year 1611, under the reign of King James of England. Thus, the name; The King James Translation.

When we consider that the groups of Englishman doing the translations **did not have use** of a Hebrew dictionary, especially one that had been converted into the English language, then it becomes more evident as to why we should study for ourselves and pray for guidance. As we are doing so, we should be grateful because **we do have access** to a Greek and Hebrew dictionary, which has been converted into the English language. It's called a Strong's Exhaustive Concordance. To make this an even bigger can of worms, the English language that was in use during the years up to 1611 was and still is evolving.

The English language changes from one generation to another. The Greek and the Hebrew languages do not evolve. **They do not change.** They are in concrete so to speak. That is why God inspired the original manuscripts to be completed in the Hebrew and Greek languages.

Next, we need to consider that the Nation of Israel did not exist in the years just prior to 1611. The Jewish people had been dispersed all over Europe and elsewhere due to military domination and the destruction of much of Israel in year 70 A D. The English translators could not contact the Universities in Jerusalem for help because the Universities did not exist yet! They could not get any help from anybody except those little flocks of Jewish people that sprung up here and there from the sojourning.

The point is that we all need to seek for ourselves in order to find, and while doing so, try to use dictionaries while we are at it. When doing so, we might have a better understanding of the words being translated than the guys leading up the efforts prior to year 1611. Who was it that said, **seek and you will find?**

Malachi 3:8-10 generates controversies that seem unending. Perhaps this is because many **people want to hang on to their money, like I did** when I was new to in-depth bible study, rather than accept the interpretation which tells us we had better return the tithe and make offerings, because **the curse of disobedience is already well under way.** A curse is about as pleasant to think about as cancer!

When an interpretation comes about like I have unraveled it in Chapters 1 & 2 of this writing, returning the tithes and making offerings is not so difficult. Better than my interpretation, are the words of God himself as He inspires Malachi to say thru his writings in verse 10, being paraphrased; **Let me prove it to you,** or; **try it and I'll prove it to you.**

What's your personal interpretation of verse 10? What do you say a **storehouse** is?

The Hebrew dictionary indicates that should have been translated **"treasury."** Again, the translators leading up to year 1611 did not use a Hebrew dictionary, because they didn't have one! **I do!** It's reference #214.

Please consider for yourself the in-depth research of this writer. That's why I financially produced this book in the first place. **So you too can prosper!** So, you can prosper big time if you stick with the returning of the tithe and making offerings above the tithe and do so on a long-term basis. If your motive is to help fund the end time harvest of souls which is occurring right now, then I suspect you will receive very pleasant surprises, soon and very soon after implementation, rather than long term.

God is not a lair. Neither am I within the intentions of this writing. Notice how I said that. *Within the intentions of this writing.* I still fib a little now and then just like all of us do, But God doesn't. **He says put me to the**

test! He says, **Try me and I'll prove it to you!** He is the one who says it, not me!

After a stewardship sermon one Sunday, I asked for forgiveness for not previously **returning His tithe.** Then I pledged to tithe for the rest of my life, He, being my helper in doing so. Many of my decisions were based on translation studies.

Not only did I return the tithe, I funded some other activities besides. Those funds were an offering but I didn't realize it at the time. **Then I hit a financial home run** and I had no idea God was involved. I thought it was because I was so smart with skill overflowing, abundant talent, ability unspeakable with brilliance bubbling over!

What happened? It hit me like a brick. My financial home run had **God helping me swing the ball bat, not me alone!**

Next, I discovered the difference between the returning of the tithe and making offerings, which message came from a knowledgeable T V preacher. Soon I learned that the blessings from the windows of heaven are prompted by the **combination of the returning of the tithe and making offerings,** not just the tithe alone. Other truths about bible prosperity came my way.

What did I do next? I mentally upped my basic pledge from 10% to 12% and sometimes gave 15% and enjoyed doing so. I did so continually, along with funding additional activities here and there that my conscience prompted me toward. Or was it God doing the prompting?

What happened? Not too long afterwards I got a promotion at work along with a pay raise of nearly 50%. Along came **more and more blips of prosperity.** It would take hours to discuss all of them. Most seemed slow and incremental but now and then a **big bump** appeared in the upward trend. Forty-some years later I've done rather well, partially prompted by translation studies.

Therefore, I'm writing this book and **self-funding the expensive process** of getting it into a hard copy format? A format that I can **hand out for free** to anybody who has an interest. To send it to T V and radio ministries to use as a fundraising item to help them pay for airtime.

Considering the blessings that will come to me from **giving the book away free,** how much do you think it will cost me in the long run? If you say, **not one dime,** then you and I are starting to get along just fine!

Much understanding came from translation studies. Now to those preachers who do not study and believe the prosperity message, and scoff at those of us who preach it, I wish they could read this portion of this book along with page 83 and tell me how this Prosperity Preacher is bogus! **I have never asked anybody to send the money to me!** My message is to send it to the causes of Jesus Christ, for the harvesting of souls. I don't need any money. I've got a pile of it! How terrible it could be for those who scoff toward us who like to proclaim the same words John proclaimed:

Beloved, I wish above all things that you may prosper and be in good health, even as your soul prospers.

He left the 99 to rescue me !

NOTES

AUTHOR'S DISCLAIMER

The writings of this volume may contain errors. I don't know where the errors are. If I knew where the errors were, I would correct them.

He left the 99 to rescue me !

NOTES

AUTHORS CREDENTIALS
and
EDUCATION

Weekly attendance of a Baptist Church circa 1950 to 1962. Not a Southern Baptist Church, but an American Baptist Church.

Continuing education from the Hilton Inn bar stools of 1967 to 1976

In 1976 a profound born again experience, conversion, a renewing of the mind, a new attitude, deliverance, a new set of marbles, salvation, a spiritual awakening, a physic change; whatever you call it, that's what happened. All are the same to me.

In 1980 to 2000, I was a Semi fat cat businessman, involved in extensive prison ministry, **not as an inmate** like I should have been **but as an Ordained Minister!**

Sometimes there is only a slight difference between the two. Author and Publisher of over 103,000 **free** pieces (over 20 tons) of self-funded Jesus centered books and booklets distributed to over 1300 prisons in America with encouragement and co-operation of Chuck Colson Prison Ministry advisers.

From 2000 to 2020, Interim Preacher for small churches in extreme rural areas, filling the gap of previous preachers who escaped or got the boot!

SEMINARY: Not me. No way. Not a chance. Thankfully zero, zip, zilch, none. With most, I wouldn't get out of the electric chair to embrace what they teach! I'd say, throw the switch, I'm safer in this chair than sitting in some of these Seminaries. Harsher comments later.

He left the 99 to rescue me !

THE END

He left the 99 to rescue me!!!!!!!

FOR I KNOW THE PLANS I HAVE FOR YOU, SAYS THE LORD, PLANS TO **PROSPER YOU,** AND NOT FOR EVIL, TO GIVE YOU A FUTURE AND A HOPE.
Jeremiah 29:11

HE SHALL BE LIKE A TREE PLANTED BY THE RIVERS OF WATER, THAT BRINGS FORTH FRUIT...... AND WHAT SO EVER HE DOES **SHALL PROSPER**.
Psalms 1;3

.....THE **WEALTH** OF THE NATIONS SHALL COME TO YOU.
Isaiah 60:5

IF THEY LISTEN AND **SERVE HIM,** THEY COMPLETE THEIR DAYS IN **PROSPERITY,** AND THEIR YEARS IN PLEASANTNESS.
Job 36:11

THE **WEALTH** OF THE WICKED IS LAID UP FOR THE JUST.
Proverbs 13:22

HE GIVES POWER TO GET **WEALTH**
Deuteronomy 8:18

ORDER FORM

For hard copies of this book, send $20, cash or any kind of check. Includes free shipping. No credit card ordering at this time. Can be downloaded from Amazon-Kindel for $10.

If ordering hard copy please print name and address clearly because I'm old; got one bad eye and can't see out of the other one!

Send to: Rev James R Whitmer
2521 NW 114th Terrace
Oklahoma City, OK 73120

For Speaking engagements or pulpit supply, especially based on this book, please call 405 751 4521. No fees or payment required if within Oklahoma. For other States, get your wallet out! Remember now, I'm a Prosperity Preacher, so I can be expensive, but you will enjoy my messages. **Maybe** they will be the best you have ever heard!